THE IRISH WOLFHOUND

THE BRIEF CHRONICLE OF 'THE GENTLE GIANT',
A LIVING LEGEND IN THE HISTORY OF IRELAND

MURIEL MONSELL BREMNER

WOLFHOUND PRESS
& in the US and Canada
The Irish American Book Company

First published in 1998 by
Wolfhound Press Ltd
68 Mountjoy Square
Dublin 1, Ireland
Tel: (353-1) 874 0354
Fax: (353-1) 872 0207
Published in the US and Canada by

The Irish American Book Company
6309 Monarch Park Place
Niwot, Colorado 80503
USA
Tel: (303) 652-2710
Fax: (303) 652-2689

Wolfhound Press receives financial assistance from the Arts Council/An Comhairle
Ealaíon, Dublin.

British Library Cataloguing in Publication Data
A catalogue record for this book is available from the British Library.

ISBN 0-86327-636-9

10 9 8 7 6 5 4 3 2 1

Editorial Consultant: Roberta Reeners
Design and Origination: Design Image
Cover Illustration: Nicola Emoe
Cover Design: Slick Fish Design, Dublin
Printed in the Republic of Ireland by Colour Books, Dublin

CONTENTS

ACKNOWLEDGMENTS

I wish to acknowledge information gathered from the following sources.

The Irish Wolfhound (John Gordon); *Irish Wolfhound Pedigrees* (Delphis Gardner); *The Dogs of Ireland* (Anna Redlich); *The Dog* (V. Shaw); *The Irish Wolfdog* (Fr E. Hogan, S.J.); *The History of Ireland* (Blessed Edmund Campion S.J.); *The Irish Wolfhound* (Capt. Geo. Augustus Graham); *An Atlas of Irish History* (Ruth Dudley Edwards); *The Encyclopaedia of Ireland* and *The Oxford History of Ireland* (Ed. R.F. Foster); *Great Folktales of Old Ireland* (Mary McGarry); *A Treasury of Irish Folklore* (Padraic Colum); *The Book of Irish Verse* (John Montague); *Octores Antiquisi* (Vol. VI); *Shades of Green* (Vol. I, Number 2, 1976); *The Irish Wolfhound Society Yearbook* (Vol. I, 1937); *Irish Legends for Children* (Lady Gregory); *The Irish Penny Journal* (1841); *The Kennel Encyclopaedia* (Vol. II); *The Irish Wolfhound* (Phyllis Gardner); *Irish Life in the Seventeenth Century* (Edward MacLysaght).

To the colleagues and advisers who have given assistance, counsel and encouragement during the writing of this brief history of the Irish Wolfhound, I would like to express my very great gratitude. In particular, I wish to thank:

Muriel Allison (Trinity College, Berkeley Library), Iris Buchanan, James J. Collins, Sgt Major Henshall (The Irish Guards, Wellington Barracks, London), Comm. Bernard B. Kelly (69th Regiment, New York City), Mrs Thomas J. McLaughlin, Kieran Nicholson (Trinity College Library), Dr Helen Conrad O'Brien (Trinity College), Capt. Adjt. Henry O'Connor (Irish 5th Infantry Battalion, Dublin), Frank Papp, Marian Papp, Professor J.V. Rice (Trinity College), William Robinson, Bride Rosney (The British Embassy, Department of Defence, Dublin), Dr Garff B. Wilson and Mairéad Donlevy (National Museum of Ireland).

For permission to reproduce photographs and other illustrative material, the publishers are grateful to Frank Fennell Photography, The Abbey Theatre, Patricia O'Mahony, The Central Bank of Ireland, The National Museum of Ireland and Brooke Givot. Thanks also to Jane Powers and Kerry Pocock for their kind assistance.

For Justin, Guinevere, Benedict and Lucy

In memory of their grandfather, James Robert Bremner

THE HISTORY OF THE IRISH WOLFHOUND

Long known as the land of saints and scholars, Ireland is also a land of legend and lore, of mystery and myth. Few countries in the western world have kept alive the colourful tales of an ancient culture with more fervour and faith than have the Irish. Even today, Irish myths and folktales of great antiquity are recounted and relived in the music, the art and the literature of the land. Just as the romance of Tír na nÓg – Ireland's Camelot – and just as the full explanation of Newgrange still challenge the mind and woo the imagination, so other legacies from early Ireland's culture offer their own individual mysteries and make added contributions to the country's singularly rich and resolute bonding with its past. Many are based on fact, and most carry a romantic patina bestowed by time. Passing from generation to generation, they were kept alive for centuries in Ireland's oral traditions, first at the courts of kings and chieftains in the early bardic/poetic era, and then by story-tellers and raconteurs (*seanchaithe*) who became the land's choristers and chroniclers and into whose keeping time entrusted its troves of facts and fables.

Among the songs they sang and the tales they told were those of an extraordinary animal – known at various times over more than a thousand years as the Wolfhound, the Great Hound of Ireland, the Grey Hound, the 'Cú', the Irish Greyhound, the Irish

Wolfhound, 'Mil-chú', the Irish Wolfdog, and even *Canes Graii Hibernici*. Renowned for his strength, famed for his courage, and cherished for his sensitivity and loyalty, he is known today as 'the Gentle Giant' – the Irish Wolfhound – of whom it has been said:

> *His history is bound up with the history of Ireland;*
> *he lived before history was born.*
> *He goes back to the mystic period of charmed romance*
> *of legend, myth and fairy tale.*
> *His name is linked with round towers,*
> *ancient harps and shamrocks.*
> *He was the faithful companion and devoted friend*
> *of St Patrick, St Kevin and St Brigid*
> *As well as that of kings, warriors and chieftains of Ireland . . .[1]*

The exact origin of the Irish Wolfhound, and the precise date and circumstance of its arrival on the island, have given rise to conjecture and controversy for centuries. It is a mystery that remains unresolved to this day. It has been held by some historians that the Gentle Giant made his appearance in Greece at the time when the Celts (Gauls) invaded and sacked Delphi in 273 BC. Reference to this theory can be found in the second-century writings of Arrian. In *The Irish Wolfhound*, John Gordon tells us that in the first century, Pliny was 'among those who praised the prowess of the hound, as had Ovid in the preceding century'. Other early Greek and Roman writers, including Arrianos, Sitius, Italicus and Strabo, praised the performance of the hounds in combat with wild animals and with armed men during the military campaigns of Roman legions. Many early drawings, as well as

---

[1] *Shades of Green*, Vol. I, No. 2, 1976.

The female figure of Hibernia, accompanied by a brace of Irish Wolfhounds

primitive bronze and stone sculptures, reproduce hound-like animals; interestingly, some are depicted as being short-coated and others are represented as having heavy, shaggier coats.

It has been suggested that the most logical antecedent of today's Irish Wolfhound reached Ireland with the Celts who arrived from the Black Sea region in the sixth century. However, in the absence of indisputable facts, this must remain conjecture. Additional researchers hold that there is even earlier evidence of the presence of these dogs in Northern Greece and Albania. While early theories may lack conclusive credibility, there can be little doubt that the hounds were in Ireland by the fourth century. Proof of this is found in *Epistolag* which quotes at least one version of correspondence between a Roman guard, Symmachus, and his brother Flavianus, in 391 AD. A letter from the Counsel thanks Flavianus, saying:

> *In order to win the favour of the Roman people for our Quaestor [Roman official], you have been a generous and diligent provider of novel contributions for our solemn shows and games, as is your gift of seven Irish dogs. All Rome views them with wonder, and fancied they must have been brought hither in iron cages. For such a gift I tender you the greatest possible thanks.*

Indeed, the feats of the hounds in various arenas, including the Coliseum, made a great impression on the Romans; it is said that on occasion, hapless Saxons who had been delegated to do combat with the hounds in the arena chose to commit suicide. As could be expected, the dogs' ferocity on the battlefield caused their fame to spread ever farther, adding to their popularity and value across the known world. Increasingly, they were presented as gifts to foreign

monarchs and to men of great influence beyond Ireland's shores. While usually given only one at a time, or in pairs for breeding purposes, the ultimate gift-beyond-price was expressed in the occasional presentation of seven hounds (in Irish lore, odd numbers have special significance).

As a result of their dispersal, it was inevitable that the Irish Wolfhound strain would come to be mingled with other breeds; in time, certain physical characteristics would alter. But the enduring, essential and distinguishing character and characteristics of the wolfhound – already so closely identified with Ireland and its lore – continued to prevail as the canine charisma of this extraordinary dog continued to set him apart from other breeds.

It is generally accepted that Ireland was the land of the Scoti when Christianity was introduced to the island. The Picts, identifiable with the Cruithore, also occupied a portion of the land for a time. The Scoti enjoyed a close affinity with a Teutonic tribe, the Belgæ, and for this reason some researchers suggest that the Belgic dog of antiquity could also have been a source from which the Irish greyhound may have developed. Later, according to the Scottish historian Major,[2] Scotland was peopled from Ireland. Considering the Irish hound's reputation even then as a hunter of large wild game – plus the fact that such game, particularly the wild red deer, abounded in Scotland – it could be assumed that Irish hounds were acquired by the Scots early on. This linking has great significance. Among early hound researchers, the work of the Jesuit, Blessed Edmund Campion, is most illuminating. He

---

[2] *The Irish Wolfhound*, Capt. G.A. Graham.

was aware that, by 1571, Irish Wolfhounds were widely dispersed, writing[3] that they had already been sent to kings of Scotland, England, France, Spain, Sweden, Denmark and Poland; to Great Moguls, Grand Turks, the Shahs of Persia; to prime ministers, various noblemen and certain 'highborn beauties'. A century later, Campion could have added the names of papal nuncios as well as Louis XIII's chief minister, Cardinal Richelieu, to this eclectic list.

The scholarly and definitive 1897 study by another Jesuit, Father Edmund Hogan,[4] provides added evidence of how the Irish Wolfhound found his home and claimed his place in the culture, the history and in the affection of the people in the land from which he took his name, carrying it with distinction and great dignity in glorious times and in times of dread and desolation; and how, like his adopted people, though tested and tried by the terrors of time, he survived. Faced with extinction and oblivion in the middle of the nineteenth century, the breed was miraculously rescued.

The Irish Wolfhound's very special relationship with his Irish masters was hard-won. From rude and rough days in caves, to places of shelter shared with monks, hermits and other early inhabitants, to the relative comfort of the castles and great holdings of chieftains, princes and the powerful, he had provided personal protection. He had led them in hunting wolves, wild boar, bears, deer and elk. When called upon, he fought fiercely on the battlefield, as he would continue to do in generations to come.

---

[3] At Turvey near Dublin (*Shades of Green*, Vol. I, No. 2).
[4] *The Irish Wolfdog*, Hogan and Graham.

He had slept at his master's side, shared his food, guarded him, his family and his household, committing himself in fealty and fidelity for life. The twin natures of the Irish hound, apposite as they are, were recognised throughout the land. According to John Gordon, Irish Wolfdogs were, at a very early date, placed as supporters of the Arms of the Ancient Monarchs of Ireland with the motto 'Gentle when stroked, fierce when provoked'.

The poet Oisian, whose works flourished in the third century, sang of the deeds of chieftains and their dogs; and whether or not his accounts have been embellished by translators down the years, his tales of the wolfhound remain part of Irish lore. The recounting of the presence of companion hounds on the ship that carried St Patrick to Ireland in 401 AD continues, as does the legend surrounding *Glún Phádraig*, emanating from the saint's encounter with a wolfhound in Ossary, as retold by Mary Reddick in *The Dogs of Ireland*.

Just as there are references to wolfhounds in the writings of ancient Greeks and Romans, the literature of other countries also acknowledges the wolfhound's presence. They are depicted in the frontispiece designed for allegorical passages from England's Venerable Bede, as produced by Sir James Ware. Further afield, the tenth-century saga of the Burnt Njal recounts that Olaf, a Norwegian whose mother was an Irish princess, presented his friend Gunnar with an Irish hound, saying:

I will give thee a hound that was given me in Ireland; he is big and no worse than a stout man. Besides, it is part of his nature that he has a man's wit, and will bay at every man whom he knows to be thy foe, but never at thy friends. He can see, too, in any man's face

whether he means thee well or ill, and he will lay down his life to be true to thee.

He then commanded the dog, so the Norwegian legend says:

Now shalt thou follow Gunnar, and do him all the service thou canst.

Thus commanded, the hound laid himself at Gunnar's feet. In time, Olaf's praise of the hound's loyalty and devotion proved prophetic, for the faithful dog was eventually slain defending his master when Gunnar was set upon by enemies. Interestingly, and as a corollary, the Irish legend of Gelert, a wolfhound which died protecting an infant from a wolf, 'is told in an old English romance; it is repeated in France; and is the subject of a Persian drama'.[5]

Through following centuries, the wolfdog remained unequalled in the hunt and in combat, renowned as a loyal companion, protector and defender.[6] The nobility was particularly attracted to him and willingly paid whatever price was asked. In 1210, England's King John presented a wolfhound to a prince of Wales. In 1336, the very young King Edward III dispatched huntsmen to Ireland to bring him wolfdogs. Wolf-hunting obviously continued as a favourite sport of other European aristocrats; in 1545, Henry VIII wrote to his Lord Deputy, instructing him to send Irish hounds to his friends at the Spanish court. Similarly, no doubt for diplomatic/political reasons, other gifts were made to kings of Sweden, Denmark and Persia. Hounds were dispatched to France as well, and in 1590, King Henry the

---

[5] The *Kennel Encyclopaedia*, Vol. VIII.

[6] A faithful wolfhound's defence of the body of his slain master on the battlefield at Aughrim (1691) is still recounted.

Great of France wrote to Ireland for wolfdogs to help him hunt wild boars. From time to time in later years, similarities between Mâtins, a large French breed, and the Irish hound were noted. But again, no definite lasting links to the wolfhound have been authenticated.

The subsuming of Ireland by the English, with its chaotic and costly politico-military and socio-economic consequences, brought on inevitable changes to the ancient, proud land. As commercial exchange between Ireland, England and the Continent accelerated, the exportation of hounds increased. This, coupled with a growing local interest in hunting wild game – not only on the part of the remaining Irish gentry (titled and untitled) but also by the latterly-arrived titled and privileged English – conspired to hasten the inevitable diminution of the wolfhound's numbers. Nonetheless, for some time, a certain number of ancient Irish castles and great houses, as well as the impressive demesnes of the resident English aristocracy, housed impressive packs of wolfhounds – a long-established custom accepted as an indication of wealth and position. Since the gifting of hounds was considered among the ultimate expressions of flattery, Queen Elizabeth I received a brace from Irish chieftain Shane O'Neill in 1562, perhaps in an effort to curry her favour and support in his struggle against the Earl of Sussex who was attempting to oust O'Neill from Ulster. A brace of Irish Wolfhounds was indeed a 'large' gift in more than one sense of the word, for Edmund Campion wrote nine years later in his *History of Ireland*:

> *They, the Irish, are not without wolves, and hounds to hunt them, bigger of bone and limb than a colt.*

9

The 'beauteous build' of the hounds was also noted in an amusing and descriptive sonnet written at the close of the sixteenth century by Lope de Vega who had allegedly sailed to Ireland with the Spanish Armada:

An Irish Greyhound of beauteous build
Bay-coloured, dark striped from head to haunch,
His collar worked in bronze with buff breast piece
Was passing by the sideway of a street.
Out sallied pellmell an army barking at him
A pack of curs, black, red and white
As from a village in fury they tear away
To pursue the wolf over hill and dale;
And, as the writers say the Moon triform
That silver orb on the celestial satin
Sets all the dogs of the mountain mad
This highborn greyhound, without heeding them
Lifted his leg, wet the projecting angle of the wall,
And through the midst of them went on quite at his ease.

In the mid-1600s, the English diarist, John Evelyn, described the vicious practice of staging combats-to-the-death between various animals in arenas known as 'Beargardens'. He also commented on the impressive appearance of the hound, recounting:

The Irish Wolfhound was a tall greyhound, a stately creature indeed, and did beat a mastiff. The Bull-dogs did exceedingly well, but the Irish Wolfdog exceeded!

Apparently much was being written about the breed during the seventeenth and eighteenth centuries. Buffon, the French naturalist, referred to the wolfhounds (which were often called 'wolfdogs' as well as 'greyhounds' at the time):

They are far larger than our largest Mâtins . . . I have never seen but one . . . when sitting quite upright [it] seemed to me to be nearly five feet high, and to resemble in form the dog we call the Great Dane, but it differed from it greatly in the largeness of its size . . . It was quite white and of a gentle and peaceable disposition.

A few years later Goldsmith, one of the famous literary figures of the time, had this to say in concluding a treatise:

The last variety, and the most wonderful of all that I shall mention, is the Great Irish Wolfdog, that may be considered the first of the canine species.[7]

He then added:

The animal, which is very rare even in the only country in the world where it is found, is [now] rather kept for show than use, there being neither wolves nor any other formidable beast of prey in Ireland to require so powerful an antagonist. The Wolfdog is therefore bred up in the houses of the great, or such gentlemen as choose to keep him as a curiosity . . . nevertheless he is extremely beautiful and majestic in appearance, being the greatest of the dog kind to be seen in the world. They were once employed in clearing the lands of wolves, which infested it in great plenty, but these being destroyed, the dogs are wearing away, as if nature meant to blot out the species when they no longer had any services to perform.

---

[7] *The Irish Wolfhound*, Graham.

Other journalists/naturalists including Brooke, Pennant and Bewick often wrote at length, lauding the beauty, bravery, vigilance, intelligence, majesty and power of the Irish Wolfdog, noting always that his numbers were dwindling. Simultaneously, the nature of the hunt across the land was undergoing change. Smaller hounds, pursuing Ireland's smaller varieties of wild game, had become the wolfhound's successor as enthusiasm for coursing steadily increased, particularly among the sporting, 'hunting-pink' clad descendants of the earlier gentry who had once followed the fleet and fierce wolfhound in pursuit of more plentiful, larger and wilder game.

Edward MacLysaght, describing Irish life in the seventeenth century, tells of visiting a household in which 'wolfe dogs' were kept. The visit is recounted in the first person and in the appropriate vernacular:

One thing I saw in this house perhaps the like not to be seen anywhere else in the world, and that was nine braces of wolfe doggs or the long Irish greyhounds, a paire of which kind has been often a present for a king, as they are said to be a dog that is peculiar to Ireland, for I am told they breed much better here than any where else in the kingdom. They were as quiet among us as lambs without any noys or disturbance. . . I am well assured that a dog of this kind which my Lord Duke of Ormond had in the Castle of Dublin when he was Lord Lieutenant, walkt into the stable yard where a little cur kept a barking and yelping at him, which he never regarded but walkt forward with a careless pace, until the cur snapt him by the heels, which made the greyhound give him a pat with his fore foot which laye him on the ground, and then standing over him pist upon him.

Pierce Charles O'Mahony, The O'Mahony of Kerry (c. 1850-1930), with his Irish Wolfhound Grania. According to a family history, 'it was from Coolballintaggart [Co. Wicklow] that he used to march to mass across the mountains clad in a green bonnet, cloak and jacket and saffron kilt, leading a leash of Irish Wolfhounds, and proceeded by a piper similarly clad'.

The exact date of the killing of the last wolf in Ireland is in dispute. The earliest purported date is 1654.[8] It is nonetheless accepted by many that it occurred in 1786 when an authenticated account records that the wolf was set upon by a pack of wolfhounds belonging to a local landowner, M. Watson, and that the incident took place in Co. Carlow at Moyshall, near Ballydarton in the Irish Republic. The event cast a long shadow across the future of the wolfhound and his destiny, joining other ominous shadows that had, in a comparatively short period (considering the country's long, long history), fallen across the future destiny of the land.

Ireland had endured much in the preceding century. As a consequence, it had changed much. The effect of the growing presence of the English and the accompanying military/political pressures which these imposed had not only brought to earth ancient titled/landed Irish families and their kingdoms and castles, so long the homes of great wolfhound packs, but it had markedly altered custom and culture.

Not only had the campaigns of Oliver Cromwell[9] indiscriminately laid waste to vast estates and splendid dwellings; they had also caused ecological devastation of an even greater significance. The great feeding and breeding grounds of wild game in the mighty forests and thickets that once rose across the mountains, hills and glens were mercilessly obliterated to meet England's commercial needs for timber, notably to build her great navy.

---

[8] Another date given is 1710. *Irish Penny Journal*, 1832.

[9] Parenthetically, it should be noted that eventually, but much too late, he unsuccessfully attempted to prohibit the exportation of wolfhounds still remaining in Ireland.

Concerning the reckless nature of the assault upon Ireland's timber, it has also been said that resident Cromwellian entrepreneurs felled vast numbers of trees, not for export, but to provide fuel for local industrial enterprises as well as to gain ready cash and quick profits. In spite of the savaging of timber-land, it was commonly thought in England that Ireland's treasury of trees was inexhaustible; while in Ireland, a poet's lamentation over the vanishing forests included these lines:

> *Cad a dhéanfaimid feasta gan adhmad*
> *Tá deire na gcoillte ar lár.*[10]
> [What are we to do without any wood?
> It's the end of the forests everywhere.]

As could be expected, the simultaneous bitter conflict raging within the country, plus economic chaos and accelerating emigration, also took their toll of men, morale and leadership; the latter was dramatically witnessed in the 1607 Flight of the Earls and the 1695 Flight of the Wild Geese. The Irish suffered numerous harrowing and humiliating military defeats towards the end of the century. Among these were the defeats at Aughrim and the Battle of the Boyne. Interestingly, the presence of wolfhounds at both of these bloody engagements has been recorded. A large-scale panoramic drawing of the Boyne battle is widely reproduced and reveals a large hound in the foreground, while the defeat at Aughrim is commemorated in a touching oft-told tale of a wolfhound which followed its master into that battle. Edward MacLysaght includes this tale in his fascinating volume on seventeenth-century Ireland.

---

[10] *Irish Life in the Seventeenth Century*, Edward MacLysaght.

After the battle, the English did not try to bury any of the dead but their own, and left those of the enemy exposed to the fowls of the air, for the country was then so uninhabited that there were not hands to inter them. Many dogs resorted to this aceldama where for want of other food they fed on man's flesh, and thereby became so dangerous and fierce that a single person could not pass that way without manifest hazard. But an Irish Hound kept close by the dead body of one who was supposed to have been his master night and day, yet he would not allow them nor anything else to touch that which he guarded. From July until the following January he stood watch over the remains of his master – leaving the scene only late at night to look for food in a nearby village. During the six months the flesh had weathered and rotted away, yet the dog still guarded the remaining 'bones'. One day, it is said, a man passing by approached too close to the remains the dog guarded, and when the animal feared the bones were going to be disturbed he charged the passer-by who, being armed, shot the dog.

This is but one of many Irish stories concerning the bravery and loyalty of the wolfhound and his ferocity when under threat. He has been identified with fighting men and military engagements over many centuries, and in several countries he is still identified not only with the military but also with national holidays and the pageantry of state occasions.

To many Irish men and women in the mid-1700s, their military defeats, plus the scope and nature of their economic and political plight, meant that the old order and character of their homeland, its former days and ways in which the wolfhound was such a fixture, were now forever changed. And whereas in the

country's much happier olden bardic times, a poet-hermit had written

> . . . *young of all things*
> *bring faith to me,*
> *guard my door:*
> . . . *wild dogs, tall deer, quiet does . . .*

another poet recalling the Celts[11] and Celtic culture had written later:

> *Great were their deeds, their passions and their sports*
> *with clay and stone.*
> *They piled on strath and shore these mystic forts*
> *not yet o'erthrown;*
> *On cairn-crowned hills they held their council-courts;*
> *while youths alone*
> *With giant dogs, explored the elk resorts*
> *and brought them down.*

Similarly, a seventeenth-century poet lamented:

> *The night sees Eire desolate,*
> *Her Chiefs are cast out of their state;*
> *Her men, her maidens weep to see*
> *Her desolate that should peopled be.*
> *Man after man, day after day*
> *Her noblest princes pass away*
> *And leave to all the rabble rest*
> *A land dispeopled of her best.*

---

[11] *Oxford Book of Irish Verse* (London, 1958), T.D. McGee 'The Celts'.

The packs are silent, there's no sound
Of the old strains on Bregian ground.
A foreign flood holds all the shore
And the great Wolf-dog barks no more.

One of many other poems mentioning hounds while
mourning the passing of Ireland's once glorious days is the epic
'Address to the Ruins of Donegal Castle'. The multi-stanza poem
relates how, in 1601, the renowned leader Red Hugh O'Donnell
reduced to ruins his great castle, once the home of mighty
wolfhound packs, rather than have it become a 'fortress for
strangers'. These random lines reflect the spirit of the epic:

O solitary fort that standest yonder
What desolation dost thou not reveal!

. . .

From there we have beheld delightful sight!
From the high pinnacles of thy white watch towers
We have seen the fleetness of youthful steeds
The bounding of the hounds, the joyous chase

. . .

Better for thee to be destroyed by thine own king . . .

Such poems were not only poignant but full of prophecy.
Despair was to be reflected in many subsequent accounts of Irish
history for at least a century. In similar fashion, despair appeared
to stalk what some felt to be the concluding chapters in the saga
of the great wolfhound. Acknowledgment of the wolfhound's
identity as a lasting symbol of Ireland is found in the 7 July 1832
issue of the *Dublin Penny Journal*. Half of the first page features an

etching entitled 'National Emblems'. The accompanying article by Terence O'Toole lists the emblems as: '. . . the Round Tower, the Wolf Dog, the Oak Tree, the Shamrock and the Harp', commenting:

> *I am bold to say, the Round Tower, and the Wolf Dog belong exclusively to our country; not so I allow the Oak or the Shamrock or the Harp . . .*

The cover design of the Dublin Penny Journal, *1832, showing a wolfhound with cropped ears. According to the text, these hounds have 'the speed of a greyhound' and the 'strength of a mastiff'. It adds that they are 'rarely to be seen'.*

O'Toole writes at some length about each of the emblems. Of the 'wolfdog' (wolfhound), he says in part:

> *. . . with paws most contemplatively crossed, [he] is looking abroad as it were, scouting with his keen round eye, for the game that, alas poor Luath! is no longer to be found on hill or curragh. Ireland, though it does indeed hold many a ravenous greedy creature, is yet no longer infested with wolves. Formerly, it was not so. So late as the*

year 1662, Sir John Ponsonby had to bring into Parliament a bill to encourage the killing of wolves. Their coverts were the bogs, the mountains and those shrubby tracts, then so abundant in the island, and some remained after the woods were cut down. The last wolf seen in Ireland was killed in Kerry in 1710 . . . the breed, though not extinct, has ceased to be common.

However, there remained for a time a few men and women who valiantly, but with diminishing results, struggled to preserve the breed which was by now so dramatically reduced in numbers and, in many instances, in size and stature.

An article on the wolfhound in the 1841 *Irish Penny Journal*'s May issue began with the following:

The Greyhound, the great hound, the graceful of limb!
Rough fellow, tall fellow, swift fellow and slim!
Let them sound through the earth, let them sail o'er the sea,
They will light on none other more ancient than thee!

The author, after praising the wolfhound and lamenting its imminent extinction, made a final plea:

Why will not some of our Irish gentlemen[12] and sportsmen turn their attention to this splendid breed of dogs, and seek to prevent, 'ere it be too late, its total extirpation?

While the message was heard, the response did not bring the desired results. To be sure, a handful of remaining landowners and hound-breeders, including Lord Altamont and the family of Sir

---

[12] Among the names most frequently mentioned are: Richardson, Rowan, Nolan, Baker, Carter, O'Mahony, O'Toole, as well as Lord Altamont, the Earl of Caledon, Sir John Browne and Sir John Power.

John Power, kept what one might consider token wolfhounds of high standard. However, the efforts of the limited number of other owners of hounds descendant from ancient and classic strains of the breed seemed insubstantial, providing small hope for the wolfhound's future.

Yet memory refused to surrender the hound's manifold ties to his homeland's history and its culture. Neither in fact nor in fable could his presence be denied, for it had been preserved for at least a thousand years in myriad images: not only on the coats of arms of the country's ancient kings, but on centuries-old manuscripts, on the treasured harp of Brian Boru, and on countless great and small recreations in stone, wood,[13] glass and metal, to name but a scattering. Memory also held enduring legends and lore that further sealed the relationship in the hearts and the imaginations of the Irish. Yeats said:

> *The Greeks looked within their borders, and we, like them, have a history fuller than any other history of imaginative events; and legends which surpass, as I think, all legends but theirs in wild beauty . . .*

Interestingly, among the most enduring of the wildly beautiful legends of which Yeats spoke are a number in which wolfhounds play a part. For instance, in the romantic tale of Dermot and Gráinne, it is told that Gráinne, the beautiful daughter of a king, was betrothed by her father to the older but powerful Finn. She

---

[13] *The Irish Wolfhound* (Phyllis Gardner) describes a tenth-century cross at Kells, for instance. The Town Sword of the ancient Irish town of Clonmel depicts a wolfhound. The celebrated Dalwey Hays of antiquity is decorated with a hound figure.

fell in love, however, with the youthful Dermot, and as a consequence the two lovers were forced to flee. Shortly, Finn and his men set off in pursuit. The tale is further complicated by the fact that Finn's own son, the young poet Oisín, had also fallen under Gráinne's spell; but so extraordinary was his devotion that he set his father's fabled hound, Bran, upon the lovers' trail, in the hope that if she (Bran) overtook them, they would recognise her at once and realise that Finn was in pursuit.

Oisín's unselfish gesture was successful. The plan worked. Bran found the pair, thus giving the necessary warning. And as if to demonstrate the hound's great sensitivity, legend says that when she finally reached him, Bran laid her head on Dermot's shoulder to convey her understanding and to offer encouragement. As with many Irish legends, the complete saga is a long one, and for that reason only a portion of it is included here.

Another enduring legend is known as 'The Last of the Fianna'. In this tale, Oisín, who figured in the preceding legend, became involved in another romantic adventure. He was pursued by Niamh, daughter of the king of Tír na nÓg, the enchanted land of Eternal Youth. To tempt him to come to the enchanted realm, she offered him the most overwhelming blandishments. Included among the bedazzling treasures in her dowry were a fortune in gold and silver – and a wolfhound!

Whereas many legends recount the deeds of extraordinary and often feared and formidable men and women, it is interesting to note the number of tales about wolfhounds in which children play an important part. Earlier, we mentioned the legend of Gelert and the fact that it had been recounted in numerous languages. It is a

tale with enormous appeal; a similar Irish tale, 'The Stolen Children', also exists. Briefly, this is the Gelert legend.

In approximately 1210, Llewellyn, a prince of Wales, received an Irish wolfhound, Gelert, as a gift from King John. The Welsh monarch had a very young princess who, according to the tale, was on one occasion left unattended except for the protecting presence of Gelert. Some versions relate that the child was an infant in her cradle; others contain illustrations representing her as being a year or two older. Nevertheless, it is always related that while the little princess was asleep, a large wolf approached and made straight for the child. Gelert sprang to the rescue, attacking and killing the beast in a bloody struggle. Soon thereafter, the prince appeared, and, not seeing the slain wolf but finding blood stains on his child and on her bed clothes, he seized his sword and slew the trusting, faithful Gelert. Almost instantly, and to his great grief, he found the dead wolf nearby and realised all too late that Gelert had killed the beast to protect the little princess.

The 'Gentle Giant'

Indeed, the legend has been so widely popular that there are numerous sketches and paintings depicting it; the following poem by Spencer recounts yet again the story of the noble hound:

The flower of all his race
So true, so brave – a lamb at home,
A lion in the chase.
'Twas only at Llewellyn's board
The faithful Gelert fed;
He watched, he served, he cheered his lord
And sentinelled his bed.
In soothe he was a peerless hound
The gift of Royal John.
Hell hound! My child by thee devoured
The frantic father cried;
And to the hilt his vengeful sword
He plunged in Gelert's side!
Vain, vain was all Llewellyn's woe;
Best of all thy kind adieu!
The frantic deed which laid thee low
This heart shall ever rue!

A second tale concerns the youthful Setanta, one of the most popular of all the ancient Irish heroes. As a result of an encounter with a wolfhound in his youth, Setanta changed his name to Cúchulainn, the 'Wolfdog of Culainn', and became known as the bravest of all first-century Irish heroes. Heroic images of Cúchulainn remain popular to this day. Accompanied by a wolfhound, he was seen on the old Irish twenty-pound note and, again with a wolfhound, as the logo of the Abbey, Ireland's

national theatre.[14] As with many classic Irish legends and folktales, the Setanta/Cúchulainn story is lengthy. His relationship with the wolfhound occurs early. Briefly, it is as follows.

Until quite recently, this was the design for Ireland's £20 bank note. It shows the poet W.B. Yeats, along with the logo for Dublin's Abbey Theatre. Created by Elinor Mansell, the logo shows Queen Maeve and her Irish Wolfhound.

In a regrettable misadventure, the young Setanta slew the wolfhound of the smithy Culainn. The lad's remorse was so great that he vowed to do his utmost to take the hound's place by guarding Culainn's house for one year. Additionally, Setanta promised to train an offspring pup to replace the hound he had killed. At the same time, he also chose to change his name to

---

[14] As created by the artist, Elinor Monsell.

Cúchulainn ('Cú' being the Irish word for hound). His new name thus meant 'the Hound of Culainn', the name he carried for the rest of his days.

Today, given the advantage of a century and a half's perspective, one could be tempted to ask how and why the wolfhound's plight went so long unaddressed. Considering that the breed was, after all, a symbol and talisman of Ireland, what sadness it must have brought many to read, at the time when Reinagle's famous wolfhound drawing appeared publicly, that the dog had 'degenerated to extinction'. With our current growing awareness of the necessity to protect and preserve endangered breeds and species, one could blame this, and other examples of disastrous and near-disastrous neglect, on the absence of requisite enlightenment at that time – the early 1800s. This is the only reasonably logical answer to the question posed at the beginning of this paragraph.

And now, there is a second question: How does one explain why the breed was so miraculously spared? The answer I offer is entirely subjective. Some would dismiss it as fanciful, while others might describe it as an Irish answer to an Irish question. Quite simply, the answer is 'the luck of the Irish'. For when the miracle required to ransom the wolfhound from extinction was most needed, fate responded. And in the nick of time, 'the luck of the Irish' wrought a miracle in the person of a Scot living in England across the Irish Sea – Captain George Augustus Graham.

Captain Graham had been active in the breeding of Scottish Deerhounds in England, and as a consequence had a wide acquaintance within the canine breeders' community throughout

the British Isles. By the time he began his wolfhound rescue mission, almost every one of the remaining specimens was considered a rarity often referred to as 'the last real wolfhound now to be found'. Many of those remaining were by no stretch of the imagination 'real' wolfhounds.

It was patently obvious to the discerning eye that the breed's appearance had changed. For one thing, the overall size of the hounds had decreased. There were a number of reasons for this,

Captain Graham, saviour of the Irish Wolfhound breed

and for other changes in appearance. Among them was the animal's relegation to a semi-sedentary lifestyle when his great hunting days were at an end. His altered diet, resulting from ecological and economic changes, was no doubt further affected in some instances by the Famine. There was also the marked modification in the once opulent style of the great Irish households which now precluded the care and cosseting of the once spectacular packs of wolfhounds. But most telling and most unfortunate of all had been the ill-advised in-breeding and incautious cross-breeding that had ensued.

Born in Scotland, Captain Graham served in the British army, eventually making his home in Gloucestershire. It was there, in 1859, that he purchased his first wolfhound. It was also from there that, three years later, the captain began his campaign, battling to rescue the faltering ranks of the Irish Wolfhound, realising that if his mission was to succeed, he would have to begin his offensive with speed and employ the best of the resources available to him. To accomplish this, Graham travelled the length of the British Isles, conferring with his many dog owner/breeder colleagues, searching out hounds and evaluating the relative merits and authenticity of the few alleged older strains, seeking always to locate, identify and ultimately use the purest lines that might still be in existence somewhere. He had no way of knowing then that he would spend the next five decades at his task, and that for a time thereafter, his son would continue his work. Nor did he know that as a result of their work, the pedigrees of 600[15] wolfhounds would have been established; and most important of all, that before he had finished his work, he would have determined, set and defined the wolfhound standards that would be followed by breeders and required by show-ring judges even to this day.

Ultimately, Captain Graham chose two of the oldest and purest known lines to be found in the Irish Wolfhound's homeland – the Ballytobin and the Kilfane. With these he began restoring the breed, doing what no one else had ever done before and, given the circumstances, what perhaps no one else could have done.

In the 1908 *Kennel Encyclopaedia*,[16] Captain Graham briefly and

---

[15] The number is an accepted approximation. *Irish Wolfhound Pedigrees*, Ed. Delphis Gardner for Irish Wolfhound Club of Ireland, 1959 (Foreword by R. J. May).

modestly reviewed his work, encapsulating its background thus:

> *Consequent on the extermination of wolves in Ireland, the number of Wolfhounds greatly decreased, and the quality greatly deteriorated as they were [by then] chiefly kept for State ceremonies.*[17]

Later in the same article, written a year before his death, he said:

> *Richardson in 1841 got together as many Irish Wolfhounds as he could and continued the breed, which Sir John Power, of Kilfane, kept up; and he, Mr Baker, of Ballytobin, and Mr Mahoney of Dromore were the last Irishmen who really tried to keep up this magnificent breed. In the year 1862, the writer took up the breed and since then, his life has been devoted to it. Fortunately, Sir John Power was a friend of his, so started with the purest possible blood of the Kilfane and Ballytobin strains.*

Captain Graham then added:

> *The present breed of Irish Wolfhounds has been built up by bitches obtained from these two kennels, crossed with the Scotch Deerhound, a very similar but much slighter dog . . . yet the writer confidently believes there are strains now [1908] existing which may be traced back more or less clearly, to the original breed.*

Graham also noted that in 1887, the ultimate arbiter, the English Kennel Club, had affixed its seal of approval on the Irish Wolfhound. With this final achievement, Graham's commitment, his work and his conviction – even in the face of inevitable set-

---

[16] Vol. II. Edited by Sidney Turner.
[17] The custom continues to this day.

backs during the decades of his careful, constant breeding, ultimately employing only the purest Irish Wolfhound lines – had at last paid off. Most of all, his faith in the ancient, noble heart and the age-old reservoirs of strength within the animal he had struggled to save were finally vindicated; and the wolfhound's future was vouchsafed at last.

In 1989, the Irish Wolfhound Club of Ireland celebrated its diamond anniversary. The occasion not only marked the long existence of the club in the wolfhound's homeland; it also provided an opportunity to acknowledge with gratitude that, due in large measure to their diligence and dedication, wolfhounds and wolfhound clubs are now to be found on almost every continent. Above all, there was tribute to be paid to the Gentle Giant, so long known as 'the greatest of the dog kind to be seen in the world'; to pay respect to the courage, dignity, strength, intelligence and fidelity of a living Irish legend, and to remembering once again that

> *His history is bound up with the history of Ireland;*
> *he lived before history was born . . .*

The writing of this small history of the Irish Wolfhound has been a labour of love undertaken for Justin, Guinevere, Benedict and Lucy, the grandchildren of James Robert Bremner, Lt. Comm. USNR, wolfhound breeder and ardent campaigner for the preservation of the breed's highest standards. It is hoped that it may also serve to enlighten those previously unaware and to remind those already informed of the extraordinary nature of the Irish Wolfhound.

Singularly identified with the history and the social and

cultural heritage of the Irish people, the wolfhound is additionally one of their rarest treasures – a living legend and talisman whose recorded presence in their midst spans almost two thousand years.

In the preface to his book *The Irish Wolfhound*, John Gordon wrote: 'No member of the Irish Wolfhound "inner circle" myself, I have written this book as a ringsider to the breed.' I, too, am not a member of this 'inner circle', but I would be remiss if I did not gratefully acknowledge friendships within it. In particular I would like to express my profound gratitude to Anthony ('Tony') Killakeen-Doyle who, apart from being a widely acknowledged wolfhound archivist-breeder-authority, gave many years of encouragement and assistance to James Bremner's Newtown Hill Kennels. I would also like to acknowledge the co-operation of two more friends from the wolfhound's 'inner circle': the author-authority Betty Murphy, and Newtown Hill's other great friend, breeder-exhibitor James Behan.

There are, of course, others to be thanked for lending encouragement and providing help and inspiration. This will be done separately. But I must mention one more person at this time – the man who approached us in the Winners' Circle one day when a Newtown Hill wolfhound had just made a clean sweep of all of the major trophies of the show, saying as he offered congratulations:

I know exactly how you feel. I've had the feeling myself. I had it when I stood in the spotlight, before thousands of people in Madison Square Garden in New York City, where my wolfhound had just been acclaimed the top winner of the US's greatest dog show. Naturally, I was proud and happy, but I knew from the instant the

cheering and applause began that none of it was for me, but for my companion, the wolfhound at my side.

So often during the writing of this I, too, have been aware of

Learning to show her Irish Wolfhound

wolfhound companions at my side, unseen, but always present. Some of them I recognised and knew by name. Some had been champions; all had been cherished. Among them, hovering closely in affection, were: Beau Flynn and Moira, Beowulf, Be Just, Banshee, Moonbeam, Benedict, Blood Axe (Buddy) and Molly. But there were thousands of others present that I had never known before. Singly, in pairs and in great packs they had arrived, gathering in numbers down the centuries as they came. Across Ireland's ageless mountains, glens, streams, fields and valleys, and

through misty thickets and the hoary hedgerows of time they had made their way here to lend inspiration and encouragement to the writing of this small chronicle. The story is theirs and theirs alone. I have been only an agent, their amanuensis, in recounting the saga of the noble Gentle Giants who, with the people of this land, have lived the history of Ireland.

The logo of Dublin's Abbey Theatre, created by Elinor Monsell, shows Queen Maeve with her wolfhound

THE STORY OF
NEWTOWN HILL
BEAU FLYNN

Under an ancient lilac tree at Newtown Hill, we buried a member of our family. His name was Newtown Hill Beau Flynn and he was a handsome, wheaten-coloured wolfhound.

We knew his parents well. His roguish father, Paul, and his mother, Moira, had lived with us at Newtown Hill for almost two years before he was born. Both of them had come into our lives under unusual and less-than-promising circumstances.

Paul, with an impeccable pedigree, had lived previously at the top of Killiney Hill within the walls of an imposing property overlooking Killiney Bay. However, at least in the eyes of neighbours, the most impressive thing about the place was the fact that by the time he was two years old, Paul (nicknamed 'Jerry' by his owners) could hurdle its high stone walls at will. Even more extraordinary was the fact that eventually, returning from his forays and forages, he could – and would – hurdle the walls again, bearing trophies and mementoes of his excursions. The trophies were many and varied, and with alarming speed they began to increase in size. The appearance of an enormous dead peacock on their doorstep caused considerable concern and embarrassment to Paul's owners. But when he presented them with an over-the-wall

*Champion Irish Wolfhound, Newtown Hill Beau Flynn,
with James Robert Bremner*

goat kid, both they and their aroused neighbours agreed that Paul's days in Killiney had to end. At the intervention of mutual friends, it was agreed that Paul would come to Newtown Hill in the hope that he would 'settle in' in larger surroundings.

Moira had come into our lives a few months earlier. She, too, had had a past filled with problems. Hers, however, were not of her making. Along with a brother who shared her splendid pedigree, Moira had been bought by a man in a distant county who fancied wolfhounds. His wife, however, preferred and bred a much smaller breed. Contention and conflict in the household ensued and the hounds were soon offered for sale. An appointment was made for us to see the male, but when we arrived, the owner's wife told us that he had been sold. Insisting in the strongest terms that we see the remaining hound, she left us for some time. When she reappeared, she was dragging a beautiful but seriously distressed female hound by a length of heavy hemp rope. It was not a pretty sight. From across the room, I could sense Jim Bremner's fury and pity at the spectacle; and I knew that though we had come a great distance to see another animal, we would be returning home with the trembling, troubled one crouching before us.

At the end of four months of care and comforting, Moira was on the way to recovering from her unhappy past. As the only wolfhound to be seen in the area for some time, she attracted considerable attention from local people who encountered her being led along nearby roads or, when freed from her lead, contentedly splashing about on her own in an adjacent canal. With the arrival of Paul, these daily routines became markedly

different. His energy and curiosity were boundless, and while the earlier walks with Moira had been leisurely, they were now completely transformed by his presence. Seemingly driven by overwhelming impatience and extraordinary surges of strength, the outings became tests of will between Paul and whoever was accompanying him.

Each day, whether along the water's edge or in open fields, he began to strain more and more vigorously at his long leather lead. Once, at a distance from his own kennel and familiar home territory, a transformation occurred; subtle at first, it became increasingly startling. He began, apparently instinctively, to hold his head even higher, as if he were listening to something far away, fixing his eyes on the distant horizon as though he had mysteriously made contact with sounds audible only to him and with vistas perceptible to his eyes alone. When he was released to run at will, we were never certain he would return.

As we watched this performance day by day, it became progressively obvious that Paul was at war with his environment. We decided then to find a new home for him, one which would provide even more space for roaming and offer more of the freedom for which he seemed to yearn. In time, we found such a place on a 600-acre farm where he could run free with other hounds.

A short time earlier, Paul and Moira had become the parents of a litter of six handsome puppies, born early on the first day of April – April Fool's Day – a day which would later assume special significance in the life of one of them and lead to the writing of this chronicle. He was the last-born of the litter and by far the

largest and handsomest of the sextet. A few days later, when he and they were registered with the Irish Kennel Club, he had been named Newtown Hill Beau Flynn.

Never having owned or bred wolfhounds before, we had done our best to learn all we could about the breed. We read books which we were told would be helpful, talked to veterinarians and hound owners, made the rounds of kennels and attended dog shows in the area. Later, we learned that we should have attended larger ones as well – in particular the Christmas holiday and St Patrick's Day events held at the RDS (Royal Dublin Society) in Dublin; both attracted huge crowds and considerable attention from the media.

In the early spring following their birth, Beau Flynn and his litter sister, Moonbeam, were entered in the Puppy Class of the wolfhound competition at the St Patrick's Day Dog Show. Amateurs that we were, we arrived at the RDS grounds with our pups like four immigrants landing on Ellis Island, and were swept along in a flood of dogs and humans who seemed to know exactly what they were about. But not us. We were adrift, overwhelmed in a tide of humans and animals. At length we were rescued. A badge-wearing official pointed us towards the show area. Someone else then directed us to a building filled with rows of straw-strewn horse stalls. Once inside, we were waved towards one of them. Completely inexperienced, we had brought no stools or shooting sticks, so we eventually sat down on the straw where the hounds had already settled themselves.

Streams of people filed past, surveying us through the stall's grille-work. And when one of them smiled and made a circle with

a thumb and forefinger in what we took to be a sign of approbation, we were puzzled. Since there were two humans and two dogs spread out on the floor of the stall, we could only speculate as to exactly which of us was getting the signal of approval.

Eventually two women stopped and spoke to us. They were from America and regularly attended dog shows at the RDS. Both were wolfhound owners/breeders. When they discovered we were complete novices, one of the women said: 'If it would be of help, I'll show one of your puppies and my friend will show the other. We'll be back in time to take them into the ring for the judging.' When they returned, each led a hound out of the stall, asking us to hide ourselves in the crowd so we could not be seen by our dogs.

The judging began. One by one, entrants were eliminated. Soon there were only three remaining in the ring – and Flynn was one of them. Then the judge nodded to our out-of-the-blue friend and handed her the first-prize ribbons. Flynn had won his first show. We had no way of knowing at that moment how many times the scene would be repeated in his future. On that day, the pursuit of champion status was not in our plans, for the simple reason that we had no plans. We were newly arrived in the highly competitive world of the show ring.

A few days later, a well-known Irish Wolfhound authority/breeder who had learned of Flynn's success asked to see him. At our guest's bidding, we walked him up and down and around and around. At length the visitor ventured a verdict: 'Nice pup, all right. He'll never disgrace you in the ring, but he'll never

be a champion.' Quite by coincidence, it was Flynn's first birthday, April Fool's Day. Thus it was with wry amusement that, a few years later, we looked at the harvest of Champion Beau Flynn's show ribbons, trophies, newspaper and magazine clippings and photographs from the show ring in Ireland and England, from national parades and civic events and films, and recalled the verdict given on his first birthday.

It is normal for owners to bond with their dogs. Even though it might seem unlikely that the commercial kennel owner, continually breeding litters, could relate with equal commitment to every animal, almost all breeders will nonetheless acknowledge that during their careers, there have been certain ones with whom they have shared a bond, remembered and cherished above all the rest. These relationships are as difficult to analyse or explain as those between humans. Because of his innate dignity, reserve and emotional stability, the wolfhound's temperament lends itself to bonding and companionship. As early puppiness fades and the bouncing, bounding boisterousness diminishes, one becomes aware that the hound has instinctively assumed the role of custodian and *chargé-d'affaires* of the humans and the household he claims. To the developing relationship he offers his affection, loyalty and protection, plus a sensitivity to the moods and emotions of the individual whose self-appointed guardian he has made himself. Because he likes activity, he will join you if encouraged. Otherwise, he will make his way to his chosen command post on the premises from which he can watch over his domain and the people he considers to be in his care. Dignity, loyalty and protectiveness have all been hallmarks of his

relationships with humans, and have been celebrated in Celtic lore for more than a thousand years.

So it was with Flynn. He set up his daytime command post beside a large stone bench under a lilac tree. From there he had an unobstructed view of the gates at Newtown Hill and of the full length of the drive leading to the house. From there, separate from other dogs and his progeny, he watched the arrivals and departures of three generations of the family, of guests, workmen and delivery men. Above all, his attention and affection focused primarily on his owner; yet he took great care to keep a watchful eye on the children in the family. Unobtrusively, with the skill of a secret agent, he moved from one area of their activity to another in his surveillance. Once when photographs were being taken of them, no one was aware of his presence until the pictures were developed and Flynn was discovered, semi-concealed, watching from behind shrubbery in the background.

His successful concealment was all the more remarkable, considering his size. Although his measurements never exceeded those considered to be the universally accepted set standards, his light colour and the thickness of his coat caused him to appear larger. On one occasion, while he and his owner were staying at a hotel adjacent to the venue for the Crufts International Dog Show in London, the occupant of an adjoining room complained to the management that the accommodation next door had a donkey in it.

Flynn was a great favourite of photographers, and on another occasion during the Crufts show, a photograph in the London *Daily Telegraph* showed him standing upright with his front legs

resting on the shoulders of a six-foot-tall man, over whom he towered.

The life expectancy for a wolfhound is approximately ten years. At the time of Flynn's death, he was thirteen years old and thought by some to be the oldest wolfhound champion in Ireland. In the company of kennel mates, progeny and the humans whose loyalty and devotion he returned in full measure, he had lived a long and eventful life.

The following year, a star was named for him. It is designated by the International Star Registry as 'RA on 22m 485d – $21°$-$56°$ in Canus Major' – the constellation of the Great Dog.

A modern champion at the Tullamore Dew Irish Wolfhound Club

THE SETANTA LEGEND
HOW SETANTA BECAME CÚCHULAINN

Dectera, one of the sisters of the High King, Concobar MacNessa, married a prince whose patrimony lay along the shores of the Muirniet, and whose capital was Dún Dalgan (Dundalk). They had one child, a boy, whom they named Setanta.

As soon as Setanta was able to understand the stories and conversations of those around him, he evinced a passion for arms and the martial life, which was so premature and violent as to surprise all who knew him. His thoughts forever ran on the wars and achievements of the Knights of the Red Branch. He knew them by name, the appearance and bearing of each, and what deeds of valour they had severally performed. Emain Macha near Armagh, the capital of the Red Branch, was never out of his mind.

Setanta saw forever before his mind its moats and ramparts, its gates and bridges, its streets filled with martial men, its high-raised dúns and raths, its branching roads over which came the tributes of wide Ulla (Ulster) to the High King. He had seen his father's tribute driven thither and had even longed to be one of the four-footed beasts that he beheld wending their way to the wondrous city. But, above all, he delighted to be told of the great school where the young nobles of Ulla were taught martial exercises and the military arts, under the superintendence of chosen knights and the High King himself.

Of the several knights Setanta had his own opinion, and had already resolved to accept no one as his instructor save Fergus MacRoy.

Of his father Setanta saw little, for his mind had become impaired and he was confined in a secluded part of the dún. But whenever he spoke to his mother, Dectera, of what was nearest his heart and of his desire to enter the military school at Emain Macha, she laughed and said that he was not old enough to endure that rough life. But secretly she was alarmed and formed plans to detain him at home altogether. Then Setanta concealed his desire, but enquired narrowly concerning the partings of the roads on the way to Emain Macha.

At last, when he was ten years old, and selecting a favourable night, Setanta stole away from his father's dún, and before morning had crossed the frontier of the Tuath (territory). He then lay down to rest and sleep in a wood. After this he set out again, travelling quickly lest he should be met by any of his father's people. On his back was strapped his little wooden shield and by his side hung a sword of lath. He had brought his ball and camán (hurling stick) of red bronze with him and ran swiftly along the road, driving the ball before him or throwing up his javelin into the air and running to meet it ere it fell.

In the afternoon of that day, Fergus MacRoy and the king, Concobar MacNessa, sat together in the park that surrounded the king's palace. A chessboard was between them and their attention was fixed on the game.

At a distance, the young nobles were at their sports, and the shouts of the boys and the clash of the metal camáns resounded in the evening air.

Suddenly the noise ceased, and Fergus and the king looked up. They saw a strange boy rushing backwards and forwards through the crowd of young nobles, urging the ball in any direction that he pleased, as if in mockery, till none but the very best players attempted to stop him while the rest stood about the ground in groups. Fergus and the king looked at each other for a moment in silence.

After this, the boys came together into a group and held a council. Then commenced what seemed to be an attempt to force the strange boy out of the ground, followed by a furious fight. But the boy seemed to be a very demon of war; with his little camán grasped like a war-mace, in both hands, he laid about him on every side, and the boys were tumbling fast. He sprang at tall youths like a hound at a stag's throat. He rushed through crowds of his enemies like a hawk through a flock of birds.

The young nobles, seized with a panic, cried out that it was one of the Tuatha from the fairy hills of the Boyne, and fled right and left to gain the shelter of the trees. Some of them, pursued by the stranger, ran round Concobar MacNessa and his knight. The boy, however, running straight, sprang over the chess-table. But Concobar seized him deftly by the wrist and brought him to a stand, but with dilated eyes, and panting.

'Why are you so enraged, my boy?' said the king. 'And why do you so maltreat my nobles?'

'Because they have not treated me with the respect due to a stranger,' replied the boy.

'Who are you, yourself?' said Concobar.

'I am Setanta, the son of Sualtam. And Dectera, your own

sister, is my mother. And it is not before my uncle's palace that I should be insulted and dishonoured.'

After this, Setanta was regularly received into the military school where, ere long, he became a favourite both with old and young. He placed himself under the tuition of Fergus MacRoy, who, each day, grew more and more proud of his pupil, for while still a boy, his fame was extending over Ulla.

It was not long after this that Setanta received the name by which he is more generally known.

Culainn was chief of the black country of Ulla, and of a people altogether given up to the making of weapons and armour. There, the sound of the hammer and husky bellows was forever heard. One day, Concobar and some of his knights, passing through the park to partake of an entertainment at the house of the armourer, paused awhile, looking at the boys at play. Then, as all were praising his little nephew, Concobar called to him, and the boy came up, flushed and shy, for there were, with the king, the chief warriors of the Red Branch. But Concobar bade Setanta come with them to the feast, and the knights around him laughed, and enumerated the good things that Culainn had prepared for them. But when Setanta's brow fell, Concobar bade him finish his game, and after that to proceed to Culainn's house which was to the west of Emain Macha, and more than a mile distant from the city. Then the king and his knights went on to the feast and Setanta returned joyfully to his game.

Now, when they were seen afar upon the plain, the smith Culainn left his workshop and put by his implements, and having washed from him the sweat and smoke, made himself ready to

receive his guests. But the evening fell as they were coming to the lios (fort), and all his people came in also and sat at the lower table, and the bridge was drawn up, and the door was shut for the night, and the candles were lit in the high chamber.

Then said Culainn, 'Have all thy retinue come in, O Concobar?' And when the king said they were all there, Culainn bade one of his apprentices go out and let loose the great mastiff which guarded the house. Now this mastiff was as large as a calf, and exceedingly fierce, and he guarded all the smith's property outside the house, and if anyone approached the house without beating on the gong which was outside the fosse, and in front of the drawbridge, he was accustomed to rend him.

Then the mastiff, having been let loose, careered three times round the lios, baying dreadfully, and after that remained quiet outside his kennel, guarding his master's property. But inside, they devoted themselves to feasting and merriment, and there were many jests concerning Culainn, for he was wont to cause merriment to Concobar MacNessa and his knights, yet was he good to his own people and faithful to the Red Branch, and very ardent and skilful in the practice of his art.

But as they were amusing themselves in this manner, eating and drinking, a deep growl came from far without, as if it were a note of warning, and after that, one yet more savage. Where he sat in the champion's seat, Fergus MacRoy struck the table with his hand and rose straightway, crying out, 'It is Setanta!'

But ere the door could be opened, they heard the boy's voice raised in anger, and the fierce yelling of the dog, and a scuffling in the bawn (enclosure) of the lios. They rushed to the door in great

fear, for they said that the boy would be torn in pieces.

But when the bolts were drawn back and they sprang forth eager to save the boy's life, they found the dog dead, and Setanta standing over him with his camán, for he had sprung over the fosse, not fearing the dog.

Forthwith, then, his tutor, Fergus MacRoy, snatched him up on his shoulder and returned with great joy into the banquet hall where all were well pleased at the preservation of the boy – except Culainn himself, who began to lament over the death of his dog and to enumerate all the services which he had rendered to him.

'Do not grieve for thy dog, O Culainn,' said Setanta, from the shoulders of Fergus, 'for I will perform those services for you myself until a dog equally good is procured to take the place of him I slew.'

Then one of the company, jesting, said, 'Cú-chulainn' (the Hound of Culainn). And thenceforward, Setanta went by this name, Cúchulainn. And he deserved it fully, for he guarded Culainn's fort for many nights as faithfully and terribly as the smith's hound which he had slain in self-defence.

THE LEGEND OF
FIONN AND OISÍN

This version of the legend appeared in an Irish schoolbook early in the twentieth century.

Fionn was the child of Cumhal, a descendant of the once-head of the Fianna of Ireland, and of Muirne, the beautiful daughter of the nobleman, Tadg. To protect the child from his father's enemies, Fionn was given at a very early age into the care of two women, one of whom was a Druid. They encouraged him in various arts but gave special attention to seeing that he learned the skills necessary for his survival in a land rife with traditional rivalries and hostilities. While still very young, Fionn left the women to join a troop of poets. In the company of the poets, the boy Fionn, we are told, wrote a paean in praise of the month of May. Random lines from the poem follow:

> *It is the month of May is the pleasant time.*
> *Its face is beautiful*
> *The blackbird sings his full song*
> *The living wood is his holding*
> *The cuckoos are singing,*
> *And ever singing.*
> *There is a brightness before the brightness of summer*

***

The harp of the woods is playing music
There is colour on the hills,
And a haze on the full lakes,
And entire peace upon every sail

***

There is a hot desire in you
For the racing of horses
Twisted holly makes a leash
For the hounds.
A bright spear has been shot
Into the earth,
And the wild flag-flower
Is golden under it.

After spending time with the poets, Fionn took service with two separate kings, leaving each in turn to continue his adventuring and his pursuit of knowledge, wisdom and the ways of the world of the Fianna.

While still quite young and unknown, he arrived at a gathering of the court of the high king of Teamhair on the eve of Samhain. Unannounced, he took his place among the chiefs at a Samhain-time feast. When asked to identify himself, Fionn replied that he was the son of Cumhal who had been King of Ireland and a leader of the Fianna, and that he had come to the court at Samhain season to seek friendship and to offer his services.

Belief in spells and magic enchantments abounded in the land.

And the most dreaded scourge and worker of malevolent magic was Aillen who, for nine years and always at this very time, had come to cast a spell over the people of the community by playing music which caused them to fall fast asleep. Having done this, he blew flames out of his mouth, setting Teamhair ablaze during Samhain. At the very time of Fionn's arrival at court, the return of Aillen was imminent and a state of anxiety was everywhere to be felt. For this reason Fiach, then the King of Ireland, rose during a court session and made a plea for a volunteer brave enough to stand guard over Teamhair and to confront the villain who was expected that very night.

None of the king's followers responded to his plea, even though, as night approached, a handsome inheritance was offered as a reward. At length Fionn volunteered. With this, the king presented Fionn with a deadly spear for his defence, and repeated his promise of reward.

Soon the dreaded Aillen appeared and proceeded to work his spell, as he had in the past. But Fionn, stripping the cover from the head of the magic spear, held it to his forehead to let its power ward off sleep. Then, pulling his crimson and gold cloak from his shoulders, he held it as a screen between him and the advancing fire. All at once, the inferno plunged downward into the earth, thus sparing not only Fionn but all of Teamhair from being consumed by flames. Thwarted, the once-dreaded Aillen attempted to flee, but was pursued by Fionn who cast the charmed spear, severing Aillen's head.

With the sorcerer's head held aloft upon the spear, Fionn returned to the court where he became leader of the Fianna. It was

said of him thereafter that he was not only a king possessed of great strength and power, but that he was also a poet, a seer and a man of wisdom. He was held to be generous, loyal and honourable, 'quiet in peace, fierce in battle'. Small wonder, then, that both he and his son, Oisín, should have shared such a close relationship with the Irish Wolfhound known even in those ancient days to be 'gentle when stroked, fierce when provoked', and that the story of Bran, the most fabled of all hounds, should be wound around the lives of these two men.

The legend tells us that Fionn's mother, Muirne, travelled to Almhuin with her sister, Tuiren. Iollan Eachtach, then chief of the Fianna of Ulster, was there also, and on seeing Tuiren, fell in love with her. When Fionn heard that Iollan was to marry his aunt, he made Iollan swear that if ever he requested it, Iollan would return Tuiren safely into Fionn's keeping. The pledge was reinforced by other members of the Fianna who had witnessed the agreement.

But the future of this arrangement held dangerous complications. For it happened that Iollan had once been romantically involved with a Druid woman, Uchtdealb of the Sídhe. Upon learning of Iollan's marriage, she vowed revenge. Disguising herself as a woman-messenger from Fionn, Uchtdealb sought out the bride Tuiren and struck her with a Druid rod, changing her into a beautiful wolfhound. When she had worked her magic, Uchtdealb led the hound to Fergus, King of Gaillimh, a man known for his dislike of dogs. On giving the hound to Fergus, the treacherous Druid woman said it was a gift from Fionn who was relying on him to take good care of the animal. Strangely, Fergus was so charmed by the beautiful hound's gentle

nature and her hunting skills that his hostility soon ended. In time, while still in Fergus' keeping, the hound gave birth to two whelps.

Meanwhile, Fionn had been told of Tuiren's disappearance. Confronting Iollan to whom his aunt had been given in marriage, Fionn demanded that a search be made for her. Iollan quickly sought the counsel of his jealous paramour, Uchtdealb, revealing that his life was in danger as a result of the pledge he had made to Fionn. Realising her lover's plight, Uchtdealb struck a bargain, saying that if Iollan would vow to keep her as his mistress forever, she would work her magic and return his wife. She kept her promise. Tuiren was restored to her human state and returned to Fionn. The two whelps which had been born to her were then given to Fionn. And their names were Scolan and Bran.

Some time later, when Fionn and a group of his men were hunting, they came upon a beautiful fawn in a wood. Seeing them, she darted away, and though they immediately gave chase, she eluded them. In time, all of the hunters and hounds retired except Fionn and his constant companions – Scolan and Bran. Eventually they saw the fawn again, but instead of attacking her, Scolan and Bran approached her in a gentle and playful fashion. As they made to leave her, she followed Fionn and the hounds all the way back to Almhuin and into the very household.

Later the same night, when Fionn was alone, a beautiful young girl appeared in his room, revealing that she had been the fawn that had followed him home. Telling her story, she explained that because she had spurned the advances of the Dark Druid of the Men of Dea, she had been turned into a deer. One day a servant of the Dark Druid, pitying her, confided that if she could escape

to some place within the realm of the Fianna, the Druid of Dea would no longer have power over her. So, fleeing as far and as fast as she could, she had arrived at the spot where Fionn and the wolfhounds had found her; and where, upon seeing her, Scolan and Bran had known at once that she was no common prey and had recognised that the three shared extraordinarily human natures.

Fionn fell in love with the beautiful maiden, who was called Sadbh, and soon married her. It is recorded that his devotion to her was enduring and absolute.

In time the Fianna, led by Fionn, were attacked by fierce enemies. A seven-day battle followed. At its end, Fionn made his way with all speed back to his wife Sadbh, who he was certain would be waiting for him at Almhuin. But when he arrived, he learned of a strange occurrence which had taken place during his absence. Tearful servants greeted the victorious Fionn and related that one evening, three wraithlike figures – resembling Fionn, Bran and Scolan – had approached the gates of Almhuin. When she saw them, Sadbh rushed to the gates with her arms outstretched, saying she was going to meet her love, her husband, the father of the child who was soon to be born to her. But the moment Sadbh's hands touched Fionn's image, its arm raised a hazel rod and with a great cry, she was transformed into a fawn. Briefly she struggled to return back through the gates but she was restrained. Just as the servants reached her, she vanished into the plain beyond.

Fionn was disconsolate and, grieving, remained in seclusion for many days. Relief from his grief came only on those occasions

when he was either hunting or making war against the foes of Ireland. Always he searched for his beautiful wife and always, when he hunted, he took only his most trusted hounds so that no harm could come to Sadbh – turned-fawn – if by chance they found her.

One day, at the end of seven years, Fionn went hunting with his men. Suddenly, there was a great cry from his own two hounds. Fionn found them circling around a handsome small boy they were protecting from the other hounds in the hunting party. The bond between the lad and Bran and Scolan was at once evident to Fionn, who also immediately thought he saw the look of Sadbh in the child's face. And forever thereafter, convinced that he was his own son, he kept the boy at his side, giving him the name of Oisín.

As a legendary poet-fighter-adventurer, his name and his father's have loomed large in Irish lore, and for centuries, stories of the bond between Fionn, Oisín, Bran and Scolan have been repeated again and again by countless generations.

Retold with frequency in this great saga is a legend saying that, many years later, Oisín, finally returning from the Enchanted Land of Tír na nÓg as an old man, found that St Patrick had come to Ireland. And upon embracing Christianity, Oisín asked if his hounds might join him in Paradise.

THE TYRONE LEGEND

This ancient tale is not among the best known of the wolfhound tales, but because H.D. Richardson's version of it, as retold exactly a hundred and fifty years ago, was presented with such story-telling charm, it follows exactly as it appeared in print in 1841.[1]

In the mountainous parts of the county Tyrone, the inhabitants suffered much from the wolves, and gave from the public fund as much as for the capture of a notorious robber on the highway. There lived in those days an adventurer, who, alone and unassisted, made it his occupation to destroy these ravagers. The time for attacking them was in the night, and midnight was the best time for doing so, as that was their wonted time for leaving their lair in search of food, when the country was at rest and all was still; then issuing forth, they fell on their defenceless prey, and the carnage commenced.

There was a species of dog for the purpose of hunting them, called the wolf-dog. The animal resembled a rough, stout greyhound, but was much stronger.

In the county Tyrone, there was then a large space of ground enclosed by a high stone wall, having a gap at each of the two opposite extremities, and in this were secured the flocks of the surrounding farmers. Still, secure though this fold was deemed, it was entered by the wolves, and its inmates slaughtered. The

---

[1] Capt. Graham referred to the tale as having come from 'the biography of a Tyrone family' (*The Irish Wolfhound*, Graham).

neighbouring proprietors having heard of the noted wolf-hunter above mentioned, by name Rory Carragh, sent for him and offered the usual reward, with some addition, if he would undertake to destroy the two remaining wolves that had committed such devastation. Carragh, undertaking the task, took with him two wolf-dogs, and a little boy only twelve years old, the only person who would accompany him, and repaired at the approach of midnight to the fold in question.

'Now,' said Carragh to the boy, 'as the two wolves usually enter the opposite extremities of the sheepfold at the same time, I must leave you and one of the dogs to guard this one while I go to the other. He steals with all the caution of a cat, nor will you hear him – but the dog will, and positively will give him the first fall. If, therefore, you are not active when he is down to rivet his neck to the ground with this spear, he will rise up and kill both you and the dog. So good night.'

'I'll do what I can,' said the little boy, as he took the spear from the wolf-hunter's hand.

The boy immediately threw open the gate of the fold and took his seat in the inner part, close to the entrance. His faithful companion crouching at his side seemed perfectly aware of the dangerous business he was engaged in.

The night was very dark and cold, and the poor little boy, being benumbed with the chilly air, was beginning to fall into a kind of sleep. When at that instant, the dog with a roar leaped across him and laid his mortal enemy upon the earth. The boy was roused into double activity by the voice of his companion, and drove the spear through the wolf's neck as he had been directed, at which time Carragh appeared, bearing the head of the other.

THE HOUND
AND THE FIANNA

Once in the glorious days of the ancient Fianna, three of its battalions arrived in Magh Femen. There three young men and their companion great hound awaited them.

From within the ranks of a forward battalion, Fionn, a fabled Fiannian, asked the three, 'From where do you come?'

'We come from Iruath in the east,' they replied. 'And our names are Dubh the Dark, and Agh the Battle, and Ilar the Eagle.'

'And why have you come?' Fionn asked.

'We have come to join your ranks and earn your friendship,' they answered.

'How will you do that?' Fionn asked.

'We will be of great value to you because each of us can provide a different service.'

'And what would those services be?' Fionn queried.

One said, 'I will do the watching for all of Ireland's Fianna.'

A second said, 'Let me bear the weight of each and every battle that challenges the Fianna's forces.'

Then the third said, 'I will overcome and destroy any challenges or threats that might be hurled at my master. I can do as much for all the men of the world. I have in my possession a pipe, the sound of which could also bring sleep to all of the men of the world.'

'As for my hound,' he continued, 'he will find food for the Fianna every second night, and on the other nights as long as deer are to be found in Ireland, I will provide it.'

'What will be your price for these services?' asked Fionn.

'There are only three things we request,' came the reply. 'First, that after nightfall, no one may come to the quarters where we live, that we alone provide for our own needs, and lastly that we are to be assigned to the worst places in the hunting.'

'By your oath now,' said Fionn, 'why may no one see you after nightfall?'

'We have a reason, but do not ask what it is. This much I will reveal: every third night, one of the three of us is dead and the other two are watching him. We do not wish to have others looking at us.'

A short time afterwards, seven poets from Cithruadh appeared in the community asking for a hundred and fifty ounces of gold and the same amount in silver for a poem they wished to write for the Fianna. The Fianna in turn felt the offer must be met, and the three young men from Iruath asked when the poets wished to be paid. They were told it would be expected on the following day. Hearing this, they called for their hound who obligingly, as the tale goes, tossed out of his mouth the requested silver and gold. Having been paid, the poets departed.

On a later occasion, on a night when the Fianna battalions had no water to drink, the three young men miraculously produced it and, for good measure, drinking horns filled with beer to finish their feasting. So merry was the evening that the place where the festivity had taken place was later called the 'Little Rath of Wonders'.

Another time, quite soon afterwards, three bald red clowns appeared, holding three red hounds in their hands, as well as three deadly spears. Their feet, their clothes and everything they touched was covered with poison. When asked by Fionn to tell him who they were, they said they were the three sons of War who in a battle with the Fianna had been killed by Caoilte, son of Ronan, and that they had come to demand a blood-fine for his death.

Fionn asked them their names, and they replied that they were: Aincel, Digbail and Espaid, also known as Ill-Wishing, Harm and Want.

'No man before me ever granted a blood-fine for a man killed in battle, nor will I give it now,' was Fionn's reply. Hearing this, the three threatened revenge and robbery. When Fionn asked the nature of the revenge they had sworn, Aincel said, 'If I encounter Fiannians, I will take their feet and their hands from them.'

To this Digbail added that he would daily kill a dog, a fighting man or a serving boy attached to Ireland's Fianna; and Espaid swore that he would always be leaving them in want of a hand, or an eye of people.

Hearing this, Caoilte said, 'Unless we get help none of us will be living at the end of the year.'

He decided to set up camp in anticipation of armed conflict with Aincel, Digbail and Espaid.

In time, the three sons of Iruath came to speak with Fionn, saying, 'It is our hope we may be allowed to let the hound we have with us circle your encampment three times a day. No one threatening to rob or harm you will have any power over you then.

But there must be no fire, no arms or any other dog in any house he goes into.'

Bearing chains of magic around his neck, the hound was sent to Fionn each day thereafter. On each day, he would circle Fionn three times and lick him three times. The three sons of the King also brought herbs to heal and help restore Fiannians who had been harmed or mistreated by the sons of Ronan.

When, in time, the High King of Ireland came to Slieve Mis with a large force to join with Fionn and the Fianna, he was told of the villainy of the sons of War and of the help that had been given by the three sons of Iruath. Having heard their story, the High King dispatched Caoilte to find the sons of Iruath, asking them to find the necessary spells to drive Uar's forces out of Ireland. This was done, and they were brought before the High King who decreed: 'Go out on the bitter sea and let each one of you strike a blow of his sword on the head of his brothers. Your harm and destruction must end.'

Following the sentencing, the hound conjured up a great blast of wind to propel the enemy into the sea where the mass slaughter decreed by the King took place. That was the last that was seen of Aincel, Digbail and Espaid. Many years later on the very day of their deaths, West Munster was visited by flocks of villainous birds from the western sea who destroyed the corn fields. They came twice again. On their second raid, they stripped trees of fruit. On the third occasion, they spared nothing living that they could lift from the ground, including small children. Once again, Caoilte worked a spell, driving the enemy into the sea.

The three sons of the King of Iruath stayed with Fionn for almost a year. Towards the end of their stay, two sons of the King of Ulster arrived. One night, while keeping watch, they made three trips around the camp. On the third trip, they saw the young men from Iruath, and their hound, encamped some distance apart. Looking closely, they observed that one of the three men was watching over the dog with a sword in his hand, and another of them was holding a white silver vessel to the animal's mouth; and any drink any one of the animal's keepers asked for, the dog would produce from his mouth.

One of the hound's keepers was heard to say to the hound, 'Well, noble one and brave one, notice the treachery that has been done to you by Fionn.'

Hearing this, the dog turned to the sons of Ulster and as he faced them, according to the legend, 'a dark dried wind rose blowing away their shields and swords, whereupon the three sons of Iruath appeared and slew them'. Eventually, searching parties were sent throughout Ireland, seeking the sons of the King of Ulster, but neither they nor their hound were ever seen again.

THE HOUND OF MASSARINE ABBEY

The Massarine legend recounts the tale of Lady Marion Clotsworthy's encounter with a savage wolf near Sixmilewater in County Antrim. It is said the encounter occurred one day in the early 1600s when she was walking in the woods near her home. Lady Clotsworthy was the daughter of Sir Roger Langford, and was the bride of the dashing Sir Hugh Clotsworthy. Sir Hugh, because of the nature of his office, was often absent from his home, and Lady Clotsworthy was frequently left alone. For diversion, and no doubt to escape loneliness, his wife often walked unaccompanied in the nearby woods. Her excursions were reportedly without incident until the afternoon she was startled at hearing the terrifying growling of a wolf close at hand.

Turning around, Lady Marion saw a huge animal with eyes of fire and distended jaws advancing upon her from a nearby thicket. Roaring as he came, the animal suddenly crouched on the ground preparing to spring upon her. Terrified, she fainted just as the beast, missing his target, over-reached his mark and fell, rolling on the ground beyond her. In a semi-conscious state, Lady Marion heard another roar issuing from a second charging animal – a giant hound – as it hurled itself past her and seized the wolf. A bloody fight between the two animals followed. Upon fully

regaining consciousness, she saw the once-threatening wolf now mangled and dying, lying prostrate on the ground. Almost at once she also became aware that close by lay a badly wounded wolf dog licking her hand. The animal had saved her life and killed his natural enemy. As soon as she could summon the strength, she made her way home again and instructed her servants to find and transport the hound to her. This they did, and with gratitude and compassion he was given great care.

Sometime later, following his recovery, the hound disappeared. It was reported that he had last been seen moving in the direction of Massarine Abbey. As time passed, the story of the wolf and the hound who saved Lady Marion's life almost disappeared and was seldom retold. However, fate eventually intervened.

During the afternoon of a dark winter's day, a sudden violent storm carrying uncommonly high winds and wild lightning plunged the entire area around the abbey into complete darkness. As the storm raged through the woods, the deep howling of a wolf dog was heard, as it again and again circled the castle's walls, sounding its warning howls. Alarm spread through the abbey and, at the direction of Sir Hugh, his warders charged towards the mound of the ancient structure. Having lit bogwood and turf fires as they advanced, they spied a heavily armed enemy lying in wait. Gunshot rang out. The enemy retreated; but as it was fleeing, a high howling cry was heard amidst the din, followed by gunshots.

When morning arrived, the warders set out to inspect the scene of the night's encounter. All was much as they expected, except for a stream of blood at the great entrance gate and a few

spent musket balls found near the side wall. But by far the most unusual and unexpected of all was to be seen on the roof of the castle. For there, in the early morning's light, they beheld, standing on the most impressive of the turrets, the wolf dog heard during the night. There he was for all to see, just as he had looked while protecting Lady Marion earlier – but now, to their astonishment, recreated in stone.

Sir Hugh, it seems, had ordered a stone reproduction made of the hound – its ears pricked, muzzle lifted, teeth bared in warning – and he cunningly seized the opportunity during the confusion and chaos of the confrontation to install the stone reproduction on the castle's roof.

Later, during a time when the castle was undergoing renovation, the stone reproduction was installed near the site where the blood and musket balls had been found. An old tradition says: 'So long as it remains there, so long will the Massarine family continue to prosper. But when it falls, then alas! for the family will speedily decay.'

THE WOLFHOUND GUIDE TO DUBLIN MONUMENTS

Elizabeth Healy

Packed with information on dozens of monuments, many of which have become so familiar to Dubliners that we have stopped noticing them. This book looks at how the monuments, memorials, statues, public sculptures and corporate art of Dublin reflect the history of the city and that of the nation.

ISBN 0 86327 637 7

THE WOLFHOUND GUIDE TO THE RIVER GODS

Elizabeth Healy

Atlantic, Bann, Barrow, Blackwater, Boyne, Erne, Foyle, Lagan, Lee, Liffey, Nore, Slaney, Shannon, Suir – these are the River Gods, the riverine heads decorating the arches of Dublin's Custom House. This book chronicles their creation by sculptor Edward Smyth and provides a short history of each of the rivers, with a description of their geography and place in Irish culture.

ISBN 0 86327 642 3

THE WOLFHOUND GUIDE TO THE IRISH HARP EMBLEM

Séamas Ó Brógáin

This is the story of one of the oldest and most distinctive national emblems in the world. From the obscurity of the thirteenth century to the present day, its history has often been concealed in myth. Now the familiar badge of the Irish State, the harp has been our most characteristic musical instrument since the eleventh century.

ISBN 0 86327 635 0

through misty thickets and the hoary hedgerows of time they had made their way here to lend inspiration and encouragement to the writing of this small chronicle. The story is theirs and theirs alone. I have been only an agent, their amanuensis, in recounting the saga of the noble Gentle Giants who, with the people of this land, have lived the history of Ireland.

The logo of Dublin's Abbey Theatre, created by Elinor Monsell, shows Queen Maeve with her wolfhound